THE PARABLES OF PRAYER

Msgr. Antonio Pitta

Preface by Pope Francis

NOTES ON PRAYER

Volume 5

Our Sunday Visitor
Huntington, Indiana

Palazzo San Pio X, Via della Conciliazione, 5 00120 Città del Vaticano
www.pcpne.va; www.iubilaeum2025.va
Published 2024 by Our Sunday Visitor, Inc.

Our Sunday Visitor Publishing Division
Our Sunday Visitor, Inc.
200 Noll Plaza
Huntington, IN 46750
1-800-348-2440

ISBN: 978-1-63966-276-0 (Inventory No. T2940)
eISBN: 978-1-63966-277-7
LCCN: 2024948713

Cover and interior design: Amanda Falk
Cover art: Adobestock

OSV extends thanks to the Catholc Truth Society for its collaboration in producing this book.

Printed in the United States of America

Contents

Preface by Pope Francis 5

Introduction 9

Jesus and Prayer 12

The Our Father: The Prayer of the Disciples 25

The Troublesome Friend and the Daily Bread 31

The Merciful Father and the Remission of Sins 38

The Widow, the Judge, and Faith 46

The Pharisee, the Publican, and the Holiness of the Temple 55

The Parable of the Fig Tree and the Approach of the Kingdom 62

Conclusion 70

Preface by Pope Francis

Prayer is the breath of faith, its most proper expression. It's like a silent cry that comes out from the heart of whoever trusts and believes in God. It's not easy to find words to express this mystery. How many definitions of prayer we can gather from the saints and masters of spirituality, as well as from the reflections of theologians! Nevertheless, it is always and only in the simplicity of those who live prayer that prayer finds expression. The Lord, moreover, warned us that, when we pray, we must not waste words, deluding ourselves that thus we will be heard. He taught us rather to prefer silence and to entrust ourselves to the Father, who knows the kind of things we need even before we ask for them (see Mt 6:7–8).

The Ordinary Jubilee of 2025 is already at the door. How to prepare ourselves for this event, so important for the life of the Church, if not by means of prayer? The year 2023 was set aside for a rediscovery of the conciliar teachings, contained especially in the four constitutions of the Second Vatican Council. It is a way of keeping alive the mandate that the Fathers gathered at the council wished to place in our hands, so that by means of its implementation, the Church might recover its youthful face and proclaim, in a language adapted to the men and women of our time, the beauty of the Faith.

Now is the time to prepare for a year that will be dedicated entirely to prayer. In our own time the need is being felt more and more strongly for a true spirituality capable of responding to the great questions which confront us every day of our lives, questions caused by a global scenario that is far from serene. The ecological-economic-social crisis aggravated by the recent pandemic; wars, especially the one in Ukraine, which sow death, destruction, and poverty; the culture of indifference and waste that tends to stifle aspirations for peace and solidarity and keeps God at the margins of personal and social life. … These phenomena combine to bring about a ponderous atmosphere that holds many people back from living with joy and serenity. What we need, therefore, is that our prayer should rise up with greater insistence to the Father so that he will listen to the voice of those who turn to him, confident of being heard.

This year dedicated to prayer is in no way intended to affect the initiatives which every particular Church considers it must plan for in its own daily pastoral commitment. On the contrary, it aims to recall the foundation on which the various pastoral plans should be developed and find consistency. This is a time when, as individuals or communities, we can rediscover the joy of praying in a variety of forms and expressions. A time of consequence enabling us to increase the certainty of our faith and trust in the intercession of the Virgin Mary and the saints. In short, a year in which we can have the experience almost of a "school of prayer," without taking anything for granted (or at cut-rate), especially with regard to our way of praying, but making our own, every day, the words of the disciples when they asked Jesus: "Lord, teach us to pray" (Lk 11:1).

In this year we are invited to become more humble and to leave space for the prayer that flows from the Holy Spirit. It is he who knows how to put into our hearts and onto our lips the right words so that we will be heard by the Father. Prayer in the Holy Spirit is what unites us with Jesus and allows us to adhere to the will of the Father. The Spirit is the interior Teacher who indicates the way to follow. Thanks to him the prayer of even just one person can become the prayer of the entire Church, and vice versa. There is nothing like prayer according to the Spirit to make Christians feel united as the one family of God. It is God who knows how to recognize everyone's needs and how to make those needs become the invocation and intercession of all.

I am certain that bishops, priests, deacons, and catechists will find more effective ways this year of placing prayer as the basis of the announcement of hope which the 2025 Jubilee intends to make resonate in this troubled time. For this reason, the contribution of consecrated persons will be of great value, particularly communities of contemplative life. I hope that in all the shrines of the world, privileged places for prayer, initiatives should be increased so that every pilgrim can find an oasis of serenity and return with a heart filled with consolation. May prayer, both personal and communal, be unceasing, without interruption, according to the will of the Lord Jesus (see Lk 18:1), so that the kingdom of God may spread, and the Gospel reach every person seeking love and forgiveness.

As an aid for this Year of Prayer, some short texts have been produced which, with their simple language, will make possible entry into the various dimensions of prayer. I thank the authors for their contribution and willingly place into your hands these "notes" so that everyone can rediscover the beauty of trusting in the Lord with humility and joy. And don't forget to pray also for me.

Vatican City
September 27, 2023

Franciscus

Introduction

After *The Parables of Mercy* (2015), which I discussed in view of the Extraordinary Jubilee of Mercy, those on prayer continue in the same vein in the year dedicated to prayer as requested by Pope Francis. The intuition on the teaching of prayer in parables comes from the evangelist Luke, who is particularly sensitive to both traits of Jesus. He is the greatest master of parables, even if it is necessary to distinguish the original source of the parables from their final version. The former is owing to the historical preaching of Jesus, the latter to the influence of the first Christian communities and ultimately to the composition of the individual evangelist. In any case, as Joachim Jeremias understood quite well, whoever delves into the parables of Jesus finds himself on a solid historical basis.

If at a certain point in His preaching one of His disciples asked Him to teach them to pray, this means that Jesus had a particular way of praying. Before Jesus, John the Baptist and the Pharisees had also taught their disciples to pray. Nonetheless, John had chosen ascetic prayer in the desert of Judah, and the Pharisees did not use parables to teach prayer. What characterizes, in a singular way, Jesus' teaching on prayer is the recourse to parables. Jesus did not invent a new system for praying. With all due respect to other masters, Jesus was not a hermit, a Buddhist monk, or a yogi. He instead chose the daily life of His people to teach prayer with parables.

In the itinerary we are undertaking, our first stop will be the prayer of Jesus and, in particular, the Our Father. Next will come an exploration of the parables explicitly related to prayer: the troublesome friend, the widow and the unbelieving judge, the Pharisee and the tax collector in the Temple, the fig tree and the kingdom of God. At first glance the parable of the merciful father, rather than of the "prodigal son," does not seem related to prayer. This consummate parable is instead meant as a response to those who object to Jesus' association with tax collectors and sinners (Lk 15:1–2). Yet the baffling humanity of the merciful father, unimaginable in any father of this world, betrays the relationship between the heavenly Father and human beings.

Except for the parable of the fig tree, which is also found in the Gospels of Mark and Matthew, the other parables on prayer are found only in the Gospel of Luke, the foremost Gospel of prayer and parables. Without wanting to force the matter, we believe that the connection between the Our Father and the parables on prayer is an original one. Jesus illustrated the

Our Father with parables, and with these He continually referred to the Our Father. This back-and-forth is decisive, between the Our Father and the parables of prayer, and so the most appropriate way to recite and explain the Our Father is found in the parables.

The beginnings and endings of the parables on prayer are not a matter of chance, but play into Luke's narrative strategy. The first parable, right after the Our Father, is that of the troublesome friend (Lk 11:5–13). The last parable concerns the fig tree, and watching for the kingdom with vigilant prayer (Lk 21:29–36). The first parable ends with the gift of the Holy Spirit (Lk 11:13); the last ends with vigilant prayer, in view of the kingdom of God (Lk 11:31). The Spirit and vigilance go hand in hand. The Spirit teaches us to pray because He cries aloud in the human soul, and vigilant prayer is born from the presence of the Spirit of Christ in the hearts of believers. It is my heartfelt wish that the readers, between the presence of the Spirit in the Church and the prayer that brings the signs of the times to light, will let themselves be guided by Jesus, the original teacher of prayer with parables.

Jesus and Prayer

Jesus of Nazareth was a man of prayer: this is one of the undeniable historical facts about His earthly life. During the few years of His public life, He often retreated in prayer, to the point that, one day, His disciples asked Him to teach them to pray (Lk 11:1). "Abba, Father" (Mk 14:36) was the shortest and most dense invocation with which He prayed. The Our Father begins with this familiar invocation: "Father, hallowed be your name" (Lk 11:2). All of the Gospels portray Jesus in prayer, Luke's more than the others at the crucial moments of His life. In prayer Jesus receives baptism in the Jordan (Lk 3:21). Before choosing His disciples He spends a night in prayer (Lk 6:12). His transfiguration on the mountain takes place during prayer (Lk 9:28–29). When He knows the end is near, despite His young age, His prayer becomes more intense: His was a true agony, a struggle that was anything but peaceful (Lk 22:44).

"Teach us to pray"

At first glance, insistence on prayer in the life of Jesus is unthinkable. What need did the Son of God have to pray so much? If He was the Son of God, did He perhaps not know the will of the heavenly Father? Between the skepticism of those who think of Jesus at prayer as in a sort of soliloquy, and the exuberance of those who see Him as simply out of this world, His was prayer in struggle, especially at Gethsemane, when He sweats drops of blood (Lk 22:44).

The author of the Letter to the Hebrews describes Jesus' prayer with realism: "In the days of his flesh, Jesus offered up prayers and supplications, with loud cries and tears, to him who was able to save him from death, and he was heard because of his reverence" (Heb 5:7). The original Greek text does not refer to the "earthly life" of Jesus, as in various translations, but to His "flesh" (*sarx*), which should rather be rendered as "humanity." With great acumen the author continues, "although he was a son, he learned obedience through what he suffered" (Heb 5:8). That of Jesus was not the routine prayer of one who was Son of God and knew everything. Rather, He learned from the suffering He endured. From "suffering," or *pathein*, He came to "learning," or *mathein*. The centuries have deposited too many layers of dust on the humanity of Jesus and His prayer, between skepticism and blasé naturalism. Between the one view and the other stands the remarkable piety of Jesus, full of humanity. What then becomes of His divine nature? If through prayer He had to learn obedience from all that He suffered, what sense does it make to consider Him the Son of God?

From the Letter to the Hebrews emerges an original perspective on the relationship between the divine and human natures of Jesus, which still has trouble getting itself across today: "And being made perfect, he became the source of eternal salvation to all who obey him" (Heb 5:9). While continuing to consider Jesus as perfect due to the exchange between His divine and human natures, the Letter to the Hebrews shifts the perfection of Jesus to the end of His humanity. Upon closer inspection, from the beginning of the treatise on the priesthood of Jesus Christ, it is confessed that "in these last days [God] has spoken to us by a Son," who "is the radiance of the glory of God and the exact imprint of his nature" (Heb 1:2–3). That Jesus was Son of God belongs to the shared faith of the first Christian communities; it is the level of His humanity that remains to be demonstrated. What is in question is not an original perfection, between the two natures (divine and human) of Jesus, but rather that related to sacrifice: of one who, through agonizing prayer, has achieved a perfect sacrifice.

At this point it is necessary to change the conception of sacrifice. In the common way of thinking, "sacrifice" consists in the deprivation or renunciation of something. In reality, in the original meaning, sacrifice consists in the transformation of what is profane into the sacred: "sacrifice" derives from the Latin *sacrum-fácere*, which should be translated as "to make sacred." In this sense, Jesus' prayer is sacrifice: transformation of the everyday and profane into the sacred and holy. One of the biggest misconceptions about prayer concerns spontaneity, that is, that it should respond to what is most natural. Who hasn't prayed at least once in his life? In reality, prayer demands diligence, training that is born from the natural condition of the human person but is nourished through the perfecting of what is profane into the sacred. With prayer, Jesus transformed daily life into perfect sacrifice to the point that, since His crucifixion, it has not been necessary to repeat any sacrifice, except for that of everyone who is united to His cross.

Places of prayer

At the time of Jesus the main places to pray in Palestine were the Temple and the synagogues. The Temple in Jerusalem was considered one of the pillars of piety for the Jewish people. Annual attendance at the Temple in Jerusalem for the main holidays, such as Passover, saw rivers of people streaming in. The evangelist Luke recalls the baby Jesus' visit to the Temple for purification (Lk 2:22–24), and at the age of twelve for the *bar mizwah* (Lk 2:42), the transition from childhood to youth. So it should come as no surprise that Jesus tells the parable of the Pharisee and the tax collector in the Temple (Lk 18:9–14), on which we will focus. Meanwhile, on the occasion of the expulsion of the money changers from the Temple, Jesus recalls the prophet Isaiah to define the Temple as a "house of prayer" (Is 56:7, in Lk 19:46).

In addition to the Temple in Jerusalem, the synagogues scattered throughout the villages of Palestine allowed prayer to continue. It is no coincidence that Luke chooses the synagogue of Nazareth to recount the beginning of Jesus' public life (Lk 4:16–30). The synagogue was a place of prayer and immersion in Sacred Scripture. With the destruction of the second Temple (A.D. 70), the synagogues remained the only places to pray in assembly. Without diminishing the function of the Temple and the synagogue, Luke notes that Jesus prayed everywhere: in the desert, on the occasion of temptations (Lk 4:1) or in isolated places (Lk 5:16, 9:18). Yet for prayer He preferred the mountains, as before choosing the disciples (Lk 6:12) and on the occasion of the Transfiguration (Lk 9:28). The place He loved most was the "Mount of Olives" (Lk 22:39), not far from the city walls of Jerusalem, beyond the Kidron valley. On that mountain Jesus sweated drops of blood, and from that place (Lk 24:50–53) He was taken up into heaven, on the occasion of the Ascension (Acts 1:12). The preference for the mountain is due to one of the features of prayer: ascesis, or upward tension. When it is authentic, prayer provides a state of buoyancy (not lightness) by which one is lifted upwards. This state is proper not only to exceptional situations of ecstasy or rapture, but to any experience of prayer. Heaven recalls the place of encounter for the one who climbs a mountain to pray.

The range of Jesus' places of prayer — from the Temple to the synagogue, from the desert to the mountain — is due to the sanctity of creation. Jesus never denigrated the Temple or the synagogue, and yet any place presented the opportunity for Him to relate to the Father. The dialogue with the Samaritan woman at the well captures one of the most original features of prayer for Jesus: "'Woman, believe me, the hour is coming when neither on this mountain nor in Jerusalem will you worship the Father. … God is spirit, and those who worship him must worship in spirit and truth'" (Jn 4:21, 24).

When religions get into arguments about the best places to pray — synagogue, temple, shrine, mosque, church — Jesus reminds us that it is not on Mount Gerizìm that God is worshiped, nor on Mount Zion, but in Spirit and truth. Worshiping God in Spirit and truth means worshiping Him guided by the Spirit who leads to the deepest truth. And the truth in question is not an idea, nor a concept, but Jesus himself: He is the truth who establishes authentic worship of the Father.

What types of prayer?

There is not just one type of prayer, but this takes on different expressions depending on the many situations. This also holds true for Jesus, who modeled different forms of prayer for His disciples: thanksgiving, blessing, praise, petition and supplication. During the Last Supper, Jesus thanked the Father twice before distributing the cup and bread to the disciples (Lk 22:17, 19). The verb chosen is *eucharisteō*, from which today's "Eucharist" derives. Before sharing any meal, Jesus and His disciples thanked the Lord for His providence.

Similar to thanksgiving is the blessing addressed to the Lord. Luke portrays Jesus in this attitude before the multiplication of the loaves and fishes (Lk 9:16) and on the occasion of the encounter with the disciples of Emmaus (Lk 24:53). The blessing of the bread must have been so habitual for Jesus that the disciples of Emmaus recognized Him as soon as He broke the bread with them (Lk 24:54). Thanksgiving and blessing express an essential trait of prayer: detachment from self and complete self-entrustment to the Lord. For this reason, even when other forms of prayer take over, such as petition or supplication, they are preceded by thanksgiving and/or blessing. The Our Father is exemplary in this regard: the first part asks that, as Father, God sanctify His name, bring about His kingdom and carry out His will. Onto this blessing are grafted the petitions for daily bread, the forgiveness of debts or sins and not allowing one to enter into temptation.

One widespread form of prayer in the environs of Palestine was praying with the Psalms. Mark recalls that Jesus and His disciples concluded the Last Supper with the song of the great Hallel, Psalm 136 (Mk 14:26). According to established Jewish tradition, this song was used above all at the end of the Passover supper because it recalled the actions of the Lord in salvation history. Jesus must have been so used to praying with the Psalms that His last words on the cross take up the beginning of Psalm 22: "My God, my God, why have you forsaken me?" (Mk 15:34; Mt 27:46).

Personal and community prayer often become petitions. Among Jesus' petitions, one that stands out is for the harvest: it is great, but since workers are scarce, He asks the disciples to pray that the Lord will send workers into His harvest (Mt 9:38). The prayer of petition denotes the state of indigence or lack in which those who pronounce it find themselves. This is why as long as Jesus is with His disciples, they do not need to fast. When the bridegroom is taken away from them, they too will fast, like John's disciples (Lk 5:33). During the passion, Jesus is concerned about the constancy of Peter's faith: He has prayed for him so that, once converted, he may be able to strengthen his brothers (Lk 22:32).

For Jesus, vigilance that becomes prayer is the means to make it through the unforeseen and be ready to meet the Lord (Lk 21:36). This is a matter of vigilance in prayer, and not of some sort of nocturnal sleeplessness. The opposite of vigilance in prayer is when one is overcome by sleep, like the disciples in the Garden of Olives (Mk 14:34–38). Jesus' prayer is so imbued with humanity that it turns into a cry when He reaches the end of His life: "At the ninth hour Jesus cried [and did not just shout] with a loud voice ..." (Mk 15:34). His was the most tormented cry, a plea to know the ultimate end for which God has abandoned Him on the cross. The final moment of Jesus' earthly life was not marked by a routine outcome, since after all He was the Son of God. On the contrary, His last breath is imbued with trust and with the cry raised by one who is in agony and holds the Father answerable.

One of the most widely known aspects of Jesus' life is His ability to perform miracles. In reality, Jesus was not the only wonder-worker spoken of in the ancient world. Alexander the Great and Apollonius of Tyana were also considered wonder-workers. Yet while other wonder-workers performed miracles and exorcisms due to their extraordinary abilities, Jesus attributes this power to prayer and, in particular, to His relationship with the Father. Emblematic is the healing of a possessed boy, whom his father has to bring to Jesus because His disciples were unable to heal him. Once the boy is healed, the disciples ask Jesus why they were unable to drive the demon out. Jesus replies that "This kind cannot be driven out by anything but prayer" (Mk 9:29). Where there is prayer, evil, and in particular "the evil one," withdraw and lose their power.

This review of Jesus' prayer demonstrates His profound humanity. There is not just one type of prayer, but this traverses all situations in life, like breathing: labored, anxious, excited, calm, peaceful, open and suffocating. In a word, Jesus' prayer is daily, like the daily bread to be asked for in the Our Father.

The contents of prayer

The evangelists have handed down various instances of Jesus' prayer; the best known is the Our Father, but it is not the only one. The "prayer of the little ones" remained so imprinted on the early traditions of the Church that it is reported among the "sayings" of Jesus: "I thank you, Father, Lord of heaven and earth, that you have hidden these things from the wise and understanding and revealed them to little children" (Mt 11:25; Lk 10:21). Greater maturity in prayer leads to greater awareness of one's smallness. The "little ones" in question are not those who remain children, gripped by a form of permanent infantilism. Rather, "the little ones" are those who become so through their relationship with the Lord. Those who have no social or political sway are on the receiving end of God's will, transmitted through revelation by Jesus.

To understand the will of the Lord in one's existence one must grow smaller, since God withdraws and hides from those who pride themselves on their intelligence. This is not to be taken as ruling out wisdom per se or intelligence across the board, but rather a wisdom that presumes it can do without prayer, considering this useless for the purposes of self-realization. When it is authentic, prayer does not become self-exaltation, but a sacred precinct of God's will revealed by grace and not by right.

Among the best-known prayers of Jesus, the invocation "Abba" stands out, related by Mark: "Abba, Father, all things are possible for you. Remove this cup from me. Yet not what I will, but what you will" (Mk 14:36). Some clarifications are necessary on this invocation, otherwise its nature will be misunderstood. "Abba" is among the "very words of Jesus" and was not invented by the evangelist Mark. This is an invocation in Aramaic, the language of Jesus and of Galilee. Most likely, this invocation spread rapidly and was imprinted in the collective memory of the first communities (Gal 4:6; Rom 8:15). Since the Our Father begins with "Father" in Luke 11:2 without the addition of the possessive "our," it follows that Jesus often addressed God by calling Him "Father." So, it should come as no surprise that in relating Jesus' broader prayer the evangelist John should insist on the invocation "Father." The recognition of the paternity of God runs throughout the stupendous "priestly prayer," related in the fourth Gospel (Jn 17:1–26). The name of God, which Jesus has made known to the world, is "Father," the expression of God's infinite love for human beings.

Yet "Abba, Father" is not a meteorite fallen from the sky but is a standard part of Jewish prayer in the time of Jesus. One of the *Eighteen Blessings*, widespread in the synagogues of the first century, is similar to the petition for forgiveness in the Our Father: "Forgive us, our Father, for we have sinned against you" (*Eighteen Blessings*, 6). The *Kaddish*, or prayer for sanctification used in the synagogue, basically begins like the first part of the Our Father: "Exalted and sanctified be His great *Name* in the world which He created according to His will. And may He establish His kingdom in your lifetime and in your days …" (Charles H. H. Wright, *The Intermediate State and Prayers for the Dead*, James Nisbet & Co., London 1900, p. 129, emphasis added).

So the idea of God's fatherhood does not belong only to Jesus. The prophets, moreover, had already recognized the fatherhood and motherhood of God. On behalf of his people, the prophet Isaiah invokes: "O Lord, you are our Father; / we are the clay, and you are our potter" (Is 64:8).

A little further on, the same prophet compares God's love for His people with that of a mother who comforts her child (Is 66:13). God's motherly and fatherly love is even more faithful than that of a mother for her child. Even if a woman were to forget her child, God will never forget him (Is 49:15). Prayer provides a glimpse of the fatherly and motherly face of God: fatherly for the security He affords; motherly for the intimacy with which He relates to His children.

One of the elements of prayer for the Jewish people is the *Shema*, the confession of the oneness of God: "Hear, O Israel: The Lord our God, the Lord is one …" (Dt 6:4). The recitation of the *Shema*, twice a day, was already practiced at the time of Jesus. When the doctor of the Law asks Jesus how he may inherit eternal life, the dialogue discloses the *Shema* of Deuteronomy 6:5–9 with the commandment of love for one's neighbor (Lv 19:18). It seems that before the time of Jesus the two commandments were quite distinct: on the one hand love for God, on the other love for others. In His preaching Jesus brought them together, since love for God is proved by love for one's neighbor, and vice versa (Mk 12:28–31). The parable of the Good Samaritan (Lk 10:29–37) clarifies, in an impeccable way, the bond between the two commandments. When there is a conflict, as in the situation of a dying person, love for one's neighbor has to come before that for God. The parables of prayer are situated within Jewish piety and the public life of Jesus, who taught His disciples to live in the world with wisdom and discernment, but above all to pray.

The Our Father (Lk 11:1-4): The Prayer of the Disciples

The parables on prayer begin with the brief section that the evangelist Luke dedicates to the topic (Lk 11:1–13). This is at the beginning of Jesus' journey with His disciples to Jerusalem (Lk 9:51), when He has been at prayer. At this juncture, one of the disciples asks Him, "Lord, teach us to pray, as John taught his disciples" (Lk 11:1). This is not the only time the prayer of John the Baptist is mentioned. Already during the ministry of Jesus in Galilee it was remarked that the Baptist and the Pharisees fasted and prayed, while Jesus' disciples ate and drank (Lk 5:33). The comparison with the prayer of John the Baptist highlights some essential features of the prayer of Jesus.

Prayer and discipleship

One becomes a woman or man of prayer by setting oneself to follow those who have already learned to pray. It is often thought that prayer is a natural or spontaneous tendency for everyone. Without denying this initial trait of prayer, which highlights its natural relationship with God, it is necessary to move from spontaneity to diligence. Otherwise, over time, spontaneity is increasingly reduced until it dries up. The countless worries of daily life get the upper hand and prayer is suffocated by anxiety about the scarcity of time. The transition from spontaneous to consistent prayer is necessary, provided that the natural attitude of prayer remains and that one enters a sort of "school of prayer" in someone else's footsteps.

The unnamed disciple who asks to learn prayer from Jesus had been drawn to John the Baptist's prayer with his disciples. Luke does not dwell much on the Baptist's prayer. It is not hard to deduce that the Baptist's disciples were fascinated by his asceticism, as he fulfilled his mission in the desert of Judah. In comparison, some features of Jesus' prayer stand out. John the Baptist and Jesus were men of prayer. However, while the Baptist embodied prayer with fasting and asceticism in the desert, Jesus conferred on prayer the traits of everyday life. For both, prayer requires diligence, constancy in following someone who is a teacher of prayer. With Jesus, prayer became daily, normal and constant. Daily, like the daily bread to be asked for in the Our Father; normal, as in any place where the need for it is felt; constant, like the breath in the lungs.

Jesus' prayer also distinguishes itself from that of some of the Pharisees, who seek to make themselves noticed when they pray in the square and in the synagogues. In truth, not all Pharisees flaunted their way of praying. For example, the Jewish leader Nicodemus did not make a habit of getting himself noticed in public and had gone to Jesus by night (Jn 20:39). However, the Pharisees always ran the risk of boasting about the works of piety they practiced: fasting, prayer and almsgiving. Jesus had many friends among the Pharisees, but He preferred to put the human person, especially the sick and the poor, ahead of any practice of piety.

So Jesus did not underestimate the importance of prayer, but made it daily and normal, to be carried out in any place: at home, on the street and while traveling. The Our Father is situated in this context and is essential for every disciple of Jesus. Let's dwell a bit on this fundamental prayer that Jesus taught, at the beginning of the journey, before recounting the parables about prayer.

From the sanctification of the name to the temptation for faith

The Our Father has been handed down in two versions, both similar and different: a longer one in Matthew (Mt 6:9–13) and a short one in Luke (Lk 11:2–4). The context chosen by the two evangelists is also different. While Matthew places the Our Father in the Sermon on the Mount (Mt 5:1—7:29), Luke moves it to the beginning of the journey to Jerusalem (Lk 9:51—19:46). Luke's narrative very likely matches the original context because, after a certain period, the disciples often see Jesus retreating in prayer and recognize its importance. The disciple's request that Jesus teach them to pray is understood only at an advanced stage of discipleship. So the Our Father belongs to the "very words of Jesus," handed down before the evangelists composed their writings. Let's look at the version of the Our Father according to Luke 11:2–4; it is less well known than the one in Matthew 6:9–13:

> Father,
> hallowed be your name.
> Your kingdom come.
> Give us each day our daily bread,
> and forgive us our sins,
> for we ourselves forgive everyone
>   who is indebted to us.
> And lead us not into temptation.
> (Lk 11:2–4)

The short version of the Our Father contains five petitions, while Matthew reports seven. The Gospel of Matthew adds the petitions concerning the divine will in heaven and on earth (Mt 6:10) and redemption from the evil one (Mt 6:13). As in Matthew 6:9–13, the Our Father in Luke 11:2–4 is divided into two parts: the petitions on the sanctification of the Name and the advent of the kingdom, in the first part (Lk 11:2); those on the life of the disciples, in the second (Lk 11:2–4). More than Matthew does, Luke selects the Our Father as the manifesto of discipleship.

The main new development with the Our Father in Luke's Gospel concerns the relationship that Jesus establishes with the parables on prayer. In fact, without any interruption, Jesus tells the parable of the troublesome friend (Lk 11:5–13), to expand on the relationship between the disciples and the heavenly Father (Lk 11:13). The relationship between prayer and parables resides in this original connection. Jesus taught prayer with parables, and the Our Father is reflected in the parables that clarify its contents. As a teacher of parables, Jesus could not have chosen a better way to teach prayer. In the next chapters we will explore this connection between the Our Father and prayer in the parables: the troublesome friend (Lk 11:5–13); the widow and the judge (Lk 18:1–8); the merciful father (Lk 15:11–32); the Pharisee and the tax collector at the Temple (Lk 18:9–14); and the fig tree with the signs of the kingdom (Lk 21:29–36). From the parables cited, that of the merciful father stands out. At first glance it seems that it does not have much to do with prayer, since it is occasioned by Jesus' practice of keeping company and eating with tax collectors and sinners (Lk 15: 1–12). In reality the father of the parable reflects God's way of acting with human beings. Among other things, in the course of the parable the requests of the two sons are destined to be corrected by the merciful father. The prayer of the younger son, who asks only to be taken back as a servant (Lk 15:21), contrasts with the arrogant one of the firstborn, who accuses his father of injustice (Lk 15:29). We will see how the parable of the merciful father develops, like the others, some features of the Our Father.

Let's get into the parables with which Jesus opens a few windows onto God's infinite fatherhood over the world. Jesus was a man of prayer and taught prayer using parables taken from everyday life. In this singular union of the Our Father and the parables of prayer, Jesus distinguishes himself from other teachers of prayer, ancient and new. He taught prayer with parables taken from daily life because either prayer is daily, or it isn't prayer at all.

The Troublesome Friend and the Daily Bread (Lk 11:5-13)

Jesus' first parable on prayer focuses on two decisive moments of the Our Father: the initial invocation, *Father* and the petition for daily bread (Lk 11:3). It is no coincidence that the parable of the troublesome friend alludes to three loaves of bread that a friend asks of his neighbor, that he may offer them to someone who has suddenly arrived in the middle of the night (Lk 11:5–8). Because of this connection, it is appropriate to specify the relative stature of the characters. The main character is not one of the three friends involved in the parable, but the *Father*, who, in the end, gives the Holy Spirit to those who ask Him (Lk 11:13).

As is usual with the parables, Jesus takes the long way round, starting with a realistic fact of everyday life: the lending of food between friends. As it develops, the parable relates some details with which it opens the eyes of the disciples towards the relationship with the heavenly Father. Prayer is not a pious illusion of one who imagines he is talking to God while talking to himself. Rather, prayer progressively deepens the relationship with God who is Father.

In an emergency situation

Many of Jesus' parables revolve around three interlocutors: Tom, Dick, and Harry! Or in personal terms: me, you and the other. The parable of the troublesome friend does not take exception to this cliché and follows the same plot. The realistic situation in the parable is an emergency. At midnight a friend goes to his friend's house and asks him for three loaves of bread, because he has nothing to offer to another friend who has just arrived on a journey.

Hospitality is sacred in Oriental culture, especially when it arises from emergency situations. Paradigmatic is the story of Abraham, who had hosted three men at the oaks of Mamre (Gn 18:1–16). This episode is also recalled in the Letter to the Hebrews, which urges believers to practice hospitality, "for thereby some have entertained angels unawares" (Heb 13:2). Prayer often takes place in situations of emergency or need: one turns to the Father when one is in need! And the Father knows well that the human heart is made like this. When one is in need, one turns to God; when the emergency is past, one forgets about prayer.

It is not easy to move from emergency prayer, dictated by necessity, to constant prayer, capable of overcoming all obstacles. The parable of the troublesome friend teaches the disciple not to limit himself to prayer out of necessity, but to achieve persistent prayer, like that of the friend who keeps knocking at the door. In order to bring this transition about it is necessary to overcome one of the main obstacles: God has other things to think about than granting the request for three loaves of bread. The response of the friend at home reflects this obstacle: he is not in a position to get up to give three loaves of bread to his friend. The house door is well locked, the children are in bed and the friend cannot get up to fulfill the request of the one knocking at the door.

The insistence on the three loaves reflects the first petition of the Our Father: "Give us each day our daily bread" (Lk 11:3). The first food one needs is bread to put on the table for oneself and others. The disciple who entrusts himself to the Father's providence needs first of all bread for sustenance. In this connection one grasps the daily nature of prayer. Since eating is an everyday necessity, the disciple asks every day that divine providence may never fail. Often the petition for daily bread in the Our Father is spiritualized with references to the Eucharist. Without diminishing the importance of the Eucharist, it would be misleading to worry about the Eucharistic bread without looking after the daily sustenance. God who is Father does not fail to give both the daily bread of mealtime and the Eucharist. Going from an emergency to the daily petition for bread is difficult, because everyone seeks to provide himself with sustenance without depending on others, not even on God.

This parable highlights how necessary it is to move from improvisation to constancy in prayer. When one reaches this condition, one is ready for any emergency. In daily life there is no shortage of emergency situations, such as that of a troublesome friend. And yet one prepares for these by trusting that God's fatherhood extends to all human beings.

The Holy Spirit and prayer

The second part of the parable switches the focus from the three friends in an emergency situation to the Father with His children (Lk 11:9–13). In prayer one must ask to receive, seek to find and knock that someone may open. Prayer is not so much necessary for God, who knows the human heart better than it does itself. Rather, prayer is necessary for the disciple, like daily bread, because it nourishes his interior life. The asking to receive, seeking to find and knocking to open are implicitly directed to God, who is a provident Father with His children. In practice the need for God is the inner engine of prayer.

In this second part of the parable, Jesus turns His attention to two foods to exemplify the relationship between the Father and His children. To the son who asks for a fish, his father will never give a serpent. Much less will the father give a scorpion to the son who asks for an egg. As such, some fish resemble serpents and it is not easy to distinguish an egg from a scorpion curled up in a ball. This misunderstanding often occurs in prayer: that God does not answer the disciple's prayer, and that instead of a fish He gives him a serpent, and a scorpion instead of an egg. In reality, the Father always answers the disciple's prayer, but He does so in His own way. What looks like a serpent is actually a fish, what looks like a scorpion is an egg. In such situations, the disciple urgently needs discernment, otherwise he abandons prayer.

The second part of the parable ends with the transition from the story to everyday life. If human beings, who are more inclined to evil than to good, know how to give good things to their children, how much more will the heavenly Father give the Holy Spirit to those who ask Him (Lk 11:13). At first glance, there seems to be no relationship between the parable of the troublesome friend and the Father with His children. What does asking God in prayer for the Holy Spirit have to do with this parable? In reality, Jesus seizes the most opportune moment to mention the Spirit in the parables. The comparison with the same passage from Matthew is illuminating, since it speaks of "good things to those who ask him" (Mt 7:11) and not of the Holy Spirit. In reality, the Spirit is the first gift that the Father lavishes upon His children; and with the Spirit He gives any other material and spiritual grace.

The key figure of prayer is the Spirit, who "intercedes for us with groanings too deep for words" (Rom

8:26). More than other areas of life, prayer is an experience of weakness: that of someone who ultimately does not even know what he should ask for. So the Spirit helps the disciple by becoming his companion and uniting himself with his breath. The Spirit is the breath of God poured into the hearts of believers (Rom 5:5).

Conclusion

The fact that the Spirit is not mentioned explicitly in the Our Father often leads us to underestimate His importance. Yet the first word of the Our Father is the invocation "Abba, Father," cried out by the Spirit in believers (Gal 4:6) and by them in the Spirit (Rom 8:15). Without the Spirit it is impossible to "cry out" (not just "invoke") "Abba, Father." Jesus taught His disciples to pray by turning to God who is Father, because from the start and until the last moment of His life He turned to God, calling Him "Abba" (Mk 14:36). In the first chapter we clarified that the invocation "Abba, Father" is used not only by the child addressing his father, but also by the adult who, in situations of emergency and agony, never loses faith in the fatherhood of God.

The first parable of prayer mentions the Holy Spirit in order that everyone may learn to breathe with the Spirit of Christ. However, the Spirit spoken of in the parable is not a spirit of divination, like the wind that rustles in the trees. Rather, He is the Spirit who establishes a trusting relationship with the Father and with Jesus Christ. The Spirit is all the more necessary in prayer, otherwise one falls into spontaneity and arbitrariness whereby everyone prays as and when he likes. He is the inner teacher who teaches us to pray with perseverance. The first level of Jesus' teaching on prayer in the parables concerns the move from extemporaneous and spontaneous prayer to constant prayer, under the guidance of the Spirit.

The Merciful Father and the Forgiveness of Sins (Lk 15:11-32)

As for beauty, some of Jesus' parables are true works of art. The "parable of the merciful father," mistakenly named after the "prodigal son," is among His most successful parables. In spite of countless readings it never loses its charm. Rereading it from the perspective of prayer is not out of place since, in fact, the parable refers to the relationship between God and His children. Most likely no parent would act like the father in the parable. The implausible traits with which Jesus depicts the merciful father refer to the relationship between God and human beings. In reality, in the merciful father's manner of acting it is God who as Father is in search of every human person.

If for the Greco-Roman world man is in search of man, like Diogenes of Sinope with the lantern in broad daylight, for that of the Bible it is God who is in search of man, even though He knows him through and through. The primordial question, "Adam, where are you?" (Gn 3:9) traverses salvation history and comes to rest in the parable of the merciful father. What teaching about prayer does Jesus communicate to His disciples with this parable? Let's look at the reactions of the two sons and the father's responses, to grasp some essential features of prayer. The perspective in which we are rereading the parable is provided by the fourth petition of the Our Father according to Luke 11:4. The disciples ask that the Father forgive their sins, so that they may be able to forgive their debtors.

"Father, I have sinned against heaven and before you"

The prayer of the prodigal son is a supplication dictated by urgency. When he is still far from his father's house, while he is feeding pigs, the younger son comes to his senses and prepares the request for his father: "Father, I have sinned against heaven and before you. I am no longer worthy to be called your son" (Lk 15:18–19). His supplication begins like the Our Father: "Father." Yet it is a plea dictated by necessity. The prodigal son comes to his senses not because he is repentant, but because he is in danger of starving to death. Not by chance, when he finds himself in front of his father the young man begins to repeat the same plea, but is interrupted by his father. The son would have liked to continue, as he had planned, "Treat me as one of your hired servants" (Lk 15:19). The son's plea reveals, in the negative sense, some essential features of prayer.

God is Father forever and His children never lose their condition. The more one advances in prayer the more one realizes that a Father awaits, faithful to His promises and to his search for man.

The turning point in the parable comes when the father glimpses his son from afar: "His father saw him and felt compassion, and ran and embraced him and kissed him" (Lk 15:20). The sequence of verbs expresses the uncontainable bliss with which the father meets his son. Prayer is an encounter with the Father who sees from afar, where no one else can see. The father sees his son from afar because he has been waiting for him since he left for a distant country (Lk 15:13). To be far from man won't do for God!

The need to overcome the distance from the son is enclosed in a verb full of *pathos*: "He had compassion." The original Greek is *esplankísthē*, the verb derived from *splankna,* the "bowels," the seat of sentiments and of the womb where life resides and is begotten. In his Gospel, Luke uses this verb full of implications three times. Jesus is moved at the gates of Nain when He sees a widowed mother crying over the death of her little son (Lk 7:13). The verb comes back in the parable of the Good Samaritan: "when he saw him, he had compassion" (Lk 10:33) for the dying man abandoned on the road. This verb reaches its climax with the parable of the merciful father. Prayer is a revelation of God's compassion for everyone: the fatherly and motherly compassion of God. The way Rembrandt represented

The Return of the Prodigal Son (1668, Hermitage of St Petersburg) hit the mark: the father's hands on the shoulders of the son are different. The right hand is feminine, the left hand is masculine, while the son buries his head in his father's lap. The lap is where God's compassion regenerates to new life the one who is enveloped in His mercy.

Maturing in prayer means realizing that no matter how much one may run to reach the Father, He runs first, more than anyone else, to meet His child. The one who embraces the other is not man who bows before God, but rather God who embraces His child. Prayer is, in the end, the kiss of God: the kiss of intimacy that erases the distance, even amid the unfathomable differences. The father's kiss in the parable resembles the kiss God gave to Moses in the steppes of Moab, according to Jewish tradition. To make Moses's separation from his people less painful, it is recounted that God kisses his soul, in the transit from earthly life to eternity. In prayer no one is ever an outsider, but always the child of a Father who envelops him with His fatherhood and motherhood, whatever the child's sin may be.

Next the father gives his son his dignity back. The father asks the servants to dress him in the most beautiful robe, to put a ring on his finger and sandals on his feet. The encounter culminates with the celebration for the son who died and has come back to life. All the actions of God described in the parable are distilled in the first petition of the Our Father, "Hallowed be your name" (Lk 11:2), which asks that God manifest His holiness by recreating a new life for everyone. Only God is capable of such compassion. From the moment of their encounter, only the Father acts and commands, while the child is clothed in the holiness of God. Before being characterized by good actions, holiness is an election that expresses the belonging of one who is holy before God. The saint does not belong to himself, but is the chosen property of God. Whatever the child's sin may be, the holiness with which the Father envelops and clothes him gives him new life.

The presumption of the elder son

The second part of the parable sees the confrontation between the father and the elder son (Lk 15:25–32). Strange to say, but the more difficult encounter for the father to handle is not with the second-born, but with the first-born, who has never left home. On the occasion of the younger's return, the elder son was returning from the countryside because he managed the family properties. After being informed by the servants about the celebration taking place, the elder son becomes furious and decides not to take part. At this point, the father decides to go out again to his elder son and entreat him. The son's response exudes hatred: "Look, these many years I have served you, and I never disobeyed your command, yet you never gave me a young goat, that I might celebrate with my friends" (Lk 15:29). That of the elder son is a presumptuous complaint, of one who insists on his right to have the father grant his request because he has always obeyed his Law.

In his arrogance the firstborn condemns his brother, with no way out, by denouncing his sin to his father. Only from his complaint do we learn that his brother has squandered his father's substance with prostitutes (Lk 15:30). Whenever one asserts rights before God, the presumption with which one condemns and judges one's brother is inevitable. In fact, the elder son refuses to forgive his brother because he is convinced that he himself has not sinned before his father. Thus the parable belies the petition of the Our Father on the remission of one's own sins through the forgiveness of those of others (Lk 11:4).

The firstborn is missing the essential: recognizing that God's fatherhood applies to him and to his brother. For this reason, the elder son never addresses his parent as "father," nor does he recognize the brotherhood that binds him to his younger brother. Thus prayer is turned into law and the acquisition of merit: one forgets that the other is one's brother and the drama of Cain, after he killed Abel, is enacted: "Where is your brother?" (Gn 4:9).

The father's response is disarming! He does not deny the right of inheritance that belongs to the firstborn. However, he asks him to take part in the celebration since his brother was dead and has come back to life; he was lost and has been found. Once again, what is at hand is the astonishing fatherhood of God, and not of just any parent. In compassion for man, God forgets everything and asks brother to rejoice at brother's return. The father reminds him of what the firstborn refuses to recognize: "This is your brother" (Lk 15:32). Thus Jesus responds to the arrogance of those who judge him for keeping company with sinners. The parable ends in an open or inconclusive manner. It is not said whether or not the elder son decided to participate in the celebration for his brother's return. The open conclusion leaves each person with the responsibility and freedom to decide, but God is always on the side of sinners and not on that of the righteous.

Conclusion

With His most famous parable, Jesus teaches how to pray by correcting the prayers of the younger and elder sons. The prayer of the second-born is rectified by the holiness with which God restores the dignity of a son to him. That of the firstborn is amended by the boundless fatherhood of God. The father does not deny the rights acquired by the firstborn, but asks him to go further: to recognize the brother who has returned from death to life. Between the plea of the younger son, born of urgency, and the acquired right of the elder son, the astonishing fatherhood of God asserts itself. God's response with the sanctification of the younger son is balanced by the reconciliation with which the elder should welcome his brother. Strange but true; God reconciles His children better than brother can reconcile with brother. This fascinating parable teaches how to pray without forgetting one's brother. Otherwise, the Father does not know what to do with a prayer that does not take on the burden of the sin of others: the remission of sins, petitioned in the Our Father, is inseparable from the behavior of one who forgives his brother the debt contracted (Lk 11:4).

This parable finds confirmation in that of the "merciful master" in the Gospel of Matthew (Mt 18:23–35). While Luke's parable is open-ended, not proceeding to the outcome of the encounter between the father and the firstborn, nor that between the two brothers, Matthew's ends with a dramatic epilogue. Faced with the servant for whom the king had forgiven an incalculable debt, but who does not forgive the debt of a servant like him, the master orders him thrown into prison for life. Commenting on the parable, Jesus adds: "So also my heavenly Father will do to every one of you, if you do not forgive your brother from your heart" (Mt 18:35). The reconciliation of debt between brothers is not optional, but obligatory; otherwise the unfortunate end of the servant who is not willing to forgive his brother's debt is inevitable. The remission of debt carried out by the master is the ultimate reason why the same between brothers is an obligatory consequence that leaves no excuse for anyone.

The Widow, the Judge, and Faith (Lk 18:1-8)

Jesus and His disciples are almost in Jerusalem, and He comes back to the need to pray without growing weary (Lk 18:1). So begin the two new teachings on prayer in the parables: the widow and the judge who does not fear God (Lk 18:2–8), the Pharisee and the tax collector at the Temple (Lk 18:9–14). Like most of Jesus' parables, this one also features three characters: a widow, her adversary and the unbelieving (and not "unjust") judge.

At first glance, this parable seems to repeat the contents of the parable of the troublesome friend (Lk 11:5–13), which we discussed in the third chapter. In reality, some original details on prayer emerge from the new parable. The Our Father offers a new key to access the parable: "Lead us not into temptation" (Lk 11:4), relating the temptation to the faith of the disciple.

Power and fragility compared

The principle of the "collision of opposites" can be applied to the parable of the widow and the unbelieving judge. Jesus brings onto the stage a widow and a judge, that is, the most fragile condition in the ancient social environment and the most powerful. At that time the loss of a spouse was a widespread phenomenon, especially among women. In fact, it was men who went to war and risked their lives on land and sea. This social situation was reflected right away in the first Christian communities, which, to deal with this emergency, introduced among other things the ministry or diaconate for widows (Acts 6:1–6). The condition of widowhood was so widespread that 1 Timothy even recalls the use of an actual register of widows (1 Tm 5:9). Unfortunately, the abuse of women belongs to humanity's history; that against widows was even more frequent. A widow had no husband to ensure her rights and was subject to frequent abuse. So it's no wonder if, to create a collision of opposites, the parable should tell of a widow who turns, with particular insistence, to the judge.

At the opposite pole is a judge who does not fear God (Lk 18:2). If widows and orphans occupied the most defenseless rung of society, judges were at the top. The power of a judge was boundless, to the point that one turned to him for any request. It is no coincidence that the judge in the parable is characterized by his unbelief: he does not fear God, as if to say "he is a nonbeliever" who wields power as he pleases. Boundless power is the dominant trait of the unbelieving judge. However, this judge also has his Achilles' heel: he is afraid that the widow will lay hands on him and give him a black eye (Lk 18:5).

The scene verges on irony: such a powerful man as a judge, at the pinnacle of his legal career, is afraid of a widow who asks him to do justice for her against her adversary. In this collision of opposites (a widow and a judge), one of the most fascinating themes of Holy Scripture stands out: justice. Prayer is the place where, more than anywhere else, one glimpses the justice of God, or what the Our Father, according to the Gospel of Matthew, calls "the will of God" (cf. Mt 6:10). In what does justice consist for Jesus? The parable reveals that God's justice does not consist in giving each his due, as with retributive justice, but in guaranteeing the rights of a weak person, like a widow. In prayer one experiences the closeness of God, who does not take the side of the judge, but of the widow. A God who has no need of impartial justice, but who with His will makes just those whom He loves. With a touching a fortiori argument that proceeds from a lesser degree to a greater one, at the end of the parable Jesus asks His listeners: "And will not God give justice to his elect, who cry to him day and night?" (Lk 18:7).

On first consideration, justice and election seem incompatible: justice should be the same for everyone, while election would concern some and not all.

In fact, this parable shows how justice without election is disembodied, and election without justice is limited. Against the idea of double predestination, between those elected for good and those for evil, God's election is achieved with the salvation of all, without excluding anyone. The widow in the parable is elect, because she is in the last place as to the protection of rights. In election, God always goes from last to first and never works in the opposite direction. Divine justice borrows the face of justification and salvation from election. Election receives from justice its proclivity for the salvation of all, no one excluded.

So the widow is elect and the unbelieving judge is unjust, while God will do justice for His elect. From the daily encounter/clash of the two comes constancy in prayer. The widow never tires of seeking the judge out every day, even if he is not a believer. In the end, the judge is cornered by the widow's insistence. Prayer teaches us to recognize the closeness of God, who is never on the side of the strong, but always on that of the weak.

Faith in the world

At first reading, it seems that the parable does not reflect any of the petitions of the Our Father. In reality, the final question on faith recalls the last petition of the Our Father: "Lead us not into temptation" (Lk 11:4). The temptation referred to is not of a moral nature, but rather fundamental: it is the temptation of one who no longer trusts God and desists from prayer. The devil or the one who always seeks to break off the relationship with the Father is particularly attuned to this temptation. So much so that at the end of Jesus' temptations in the desert, Luke notes: "And when the devil had ended every temptation, he departed from him until an opportune time" (Lk 4:13). The *kairos* or opportune time is that of the agony on the Mount of Olives, when Jesus asks the disciples to pray with Him to not enter into temptation (Lk 22:39–46). It is not by chance that the longer version of the Our Father, in Matthew 6:13, adds: "but deliver us from evil" (Mt 6:13).

Unfortunately, the translation of the Our Father in contemporary language does not give a good idea of the last petition. The original Greek does not use the verb "to abandon" (in Greek *kataleipō*), but rather "to let in" (*eisferō*), nor does it speak of evil in the abstract, but of the "evil one," who is the tempter or the devil. The underlying image is an everyday one, as is typical of Jesus' preaching. To understand it one must imagine a fishing trap, which at sea or on a lake, as in Galilee, is used to catch fish. Once the fish are inside, the trap door closes and they cannot get out. In a similar way, the disciple asks the Father not to be put in a position to enter into temptation; and if he has been captured there, he begs to be redeemed from the evil one. God, as Father, is asked to redeem those who cannot free themselves from the temptation of the evil one on their own. God is like the nearest relative who is expected to make every effort to keep his family member from ending up in a condition of slavery. But if this does happen, the responsibility to ransom or redeem from the evil one falls on Him. Therefore the temptation alluded to in both Luke 11:4 and Matthew 6:13 is that of faith: the same faith with which the parable of the widow and the judge ends: "Nevertheless, when the Son of man comes, will he find faith on earth?" (Lk 18:8).

The original Greek term for "faith" is *pistis,* which in turn refers to the Hebrew *emunah*, a term with different facets. Faith is, at the same time, fidelity, reliability, trust, reliance and credibility; it is not reduced to the contents to be believed but involves the relationship with the Other. In practice, the faith that Jesus asks of the disciple until His return is the trust that the Lord is on his side and does not forget that He is the nearest relative who looks out for the one who doesn't manage to come out of the temptation against faith. When it is true, prayer requires perseverance and, in any case, produces weariness in the one who must struggle. Prayer is a struggle, a contest that often leads to surrender. This is why the parable ends with the question about the presence of faith until the end.

Salvation history presents two essential paradigms of faith as understood in this way: Abraham and Jesus of Nazareth. The father of faith is Abraham, who "believed the Lord, and he counted it to him as righteousness" (Gen 15:6). He had just received the promise of descendants as numerous as the sand of the seashore and the stars in the sky. But after finally receiving Isaac, the son of the promise, Abraham is put to the test when he is asked to sacrifice this same son (Gn 22:1–19). A terrible test that Abraham endures with trust in Him who never fails to keep His promises. The liberation of Isaac, at the culminating moment of the test, confirms that it is not enough to have faith without going through the test that this entails. And so Abraham becomes the father in faith (Rom 4:1) of all those who, like him, continue to persevere in the face of trial.

Likewise decisive is the faith of Jesus, put to the test in the days of his humanity, as the Letter to the Hebrews recalls: "Jesus offered up prayers and supplications, with loud cries and tears, to him who was able to save him from death, and he was heard because of his reverence." (Heb 5:7). Thus the crucial moment of Jesus' life is recalled: the agony of Gethsemane, before the crucifixion. We looked at the faith/fidelity of Jesus in the first chapter of our itinerary. It seems that Jesus was not heard by God, because He had asked to be spared from the test. Yet He never lost His trust in the Father and abandoned himself to His will. The connection between "Abba, Father" in Mark 14:36, and "to what end [not why] have you abandoned me" in Mark 15:34 is incredible, but real. Jesus does not ask the reason for His abandonment on the cross, but rather the ultimate end. Jesus' prayer on the cross is owing to this profound relationship: "Father, into your hands I commit my spirit" (Lk 23:46). Prayer is a no-holds-barred struggle that leads to an either/or between surrendering and trusting in God, despite the apparent evidence to the contrary.

Conclusion

The Letter to the Hebrews raises a stupendous hymn to faith (Heb 11:1–40), understood as "the assurance of things hoped for, the conviction of things not seen" (v. 1). The list of witnesses of faith starts with Abel (v. 4) and ends with "a cloud of witnesses" (12:1). The history of salvation that runs through the Bible is, among other things, the history of faith: the encounter between God's faithfulness to His promises and the trust in those who do not give up under trial.

The Letter to the Hebrews is original for where it situates the beginning of faith: not with Abraham, but with Abel, since faith itself is sacrifice, conceived of not as the privation of something but as the transformation of the profane into the sacred. In this, the believer's prayer is distinctive because it does not *anticipate* sacrifice, but rather *is* a sacrifice of praise. God does not need the sacrifice of Isaac, nor the sacrifice of the Son, but from those who follow in the footsteps of Abraham He gladly receives the sacrifice of faith offered in prayer. The more one is united with Christ, through the Spirit, the more prayer is turned into a sacrifice of praise.

The parable of the widow and the judge does not limit itself to insisting on perseverance in prayer; it adds the essential purpose of prayer: to grow in faith, especially in the face of the temptation to believe that one is not heard. At the beginning of the parable, the widow is weaker than the judge: an adversary has wronged her. At the end, she is stronger than the judge, because she receives what she insistently asked for. Prayer transforms weakness into strength because it is upheld by grace: "My grace is sufficient for you, for my power is made perfect in weakness" (2 Cor 12:9).

The Pharisee, the Tax Collector, and the Holiness of the Temple (Lk 18:9-14)

In open contrast with the parable of the widow and the judge, Jesus continues with prayer in the parables, proceeding to the Pharisee and the tax collector at the Temple. This parable too is found only in the Gospel of Luke, confirming the teaching of prayer in parables. The two parables of prayer in Luke 18:1–14 are connected by the theme of justice. The justice that the widow expects from the unbelieving judge is contrasted with that of those who cherish their conviction of being righteous before God and despise others.

As with the other parables, the Our Father introduces the main key of interpretation for the new parable: "Hallowed be your name" (Lk 11:2). The petition comes back at the conclusion of the parable with the paradoxical reversal of the situation by which God justifies the tax collector instead of the Pharisee in the Temple (Lk 18:14). To get an idea of the decisive impact of the first petition in the Our Father on the Pharisee and the tax collector in the Temple, one should revisit the calling of the prophet Isaiah in the Temple (Is 6:1–9). The prophet contemplates, in a vision, the presence of God, confesses Him "holy" three times, recognizes his own impurity, and his sin is expiated. The Pharisee and the tax collector at the Temple express by contrast the positive and negative expiation of the justification that God achieves with His sanctification. God is holy because He sanctifies the sinner or the one who acknowledges his guilt, while he who does not need to be sanctified is indeed a sinner.

Arrogant prayer

As with Isaiah's vision, the parable of the Pharisee and the tax collector takes place in the Temple. At the time of Jesus, the Temple in Jerusalem was still flourishing: it was one of the cornerstones of Jewish piety. The setting of the parable in the Temple is not by chance, since the Pharisee and the tax collector pray in the presence of God, but with opposite attitudes. So this parable also has three interlocutors and not two: the Pharisee, the tax collector and God, who intervenes in the end by justifying or, according to the petition of the Our Father, "hallowing" the tax collector and not the Pharisee.

Before focusing on the Pharisee's prayer, it is necessary to dispel a few misunderstandings. At the time of Jesus, the movement of the Pharisees was the most widespread in Palestine. Jesus himself had some friends among the Pharisees, like Simon, who hosted Him at his home (Lk 7:36–50). The distinctive features of Pharisaism included faith in the resurrection and in the will of God, and domestic prayer. Jesus does not intend to make a blanket condemnation of the most important movement of His time. He instead warns against a danger common to all: becoming so used to familiarity with God as to take His place, seizing hold of the reins of justice. If it still holds true that it is necessary to move from prayer in fits and starts, offered only for personal interests, to that which is constant and capable of fidelity, the opposite danger also threatens: that of taking God's place and judging others, to the point of condemning them. To forcefully counteract this danger, Jesus sets forth the prayers of the Pharisee and the tax collector.

The way in which Jesus characterizes the Pharisee is exemplary. He portrays the Pharisee as he stands before God and pours out inordinate self-praise (Lk 18:11–12). In reality, the Pharisee's speech is a blather of thirty-three words, without pause. The self-praise begins with thanksgiving to God on no other grounds than comparison with others. The Pharisee is not like the rest, branded as thieves, unjust and adulterers. Among those he continues to judge without mercy is the tax collector who is praying at a respectful distance. That Pharisee is a guarantor of the Law: he fasts twice a week and pays tithes on all his income. So at first glance his is a commendable relationship with God and with others. Yet the negative comparison with other men and with the tax collector isolates him from relationship with his neighbor and with God. His is such an arrogant prayer that, while he presumes himself impeccable, he will return home without being justified (Lk 18:14). The reversal of the situation created by Jesus is noteworthy. The Pharisee starts from the presumption of being just, despising others, and ends up without justification. As if to say, the arrogant prayer of one who puts himself in God's place is harmful because that Pharisee idolizes himself instead of worshiping God.

The risk of idolatry is always lurking in prayer, as in life. Its most subtle form occurs when prayer is imbued with an egotism that leaves no room for God or neighbor. Indeed, the self-idolater is recognized in his tendency to despise his neighbor, to the point of condemning him. In the outraged mind of the Pharisee, the tax collector has no excuse whatsoever: he is condemned even if only for his work of collecting taxes on behalf of the imperial government. Thus the Pharisee "does not forgive any debt to his debtor," coming into conflict with the last invocation of the Our Father, according to the Gospel of Luke. Ultimately the Pharisee in the parable is neither justified nor sanctified by God because in condemning the tax collector he condemns himself and profanes the house of God, which the Temple is.

Sincere prayer

"But the tax collector, standing far off, would not even lift up his eyes to heaven, but beat his breast, saying, 'God, be merciful to me a sinner!'" (Lk 18:13). Against the thirty-three words of the Pharisee, Jesus puts seven in the mouth of the publican. And while the Pharisee stands upright before God, the publican does not have the courage to raise his gaze towards heaven: he beats his breast, acknowledging his guilt.

The tax collector could have put forward various excuses to find a loophole of justification. He was most likely constrained to carry out one of the most impure occupations of the time — collecting taxes — to support himself and his family. In reality, the tax collector does not claim any rights, but presents himself before the Lord as he is: in the nakedness of one who knows he cannot hide anything before God. It is no coincidence that his prayer recalls the vision of the prophet Isaiah in the Temple: "Your guilt is taken away, and your sin atoned for" (Is 6:7). And God, who does not consider looks or appearances, recognizes the repentant heart of the tax collector. Prayer is not just made up of words, but is characterized above all as a way of presenting oneself before the Lord. The actions of the tax collector who stands off at a distance, does not allow himself to look up to heaven and beats his breast, are already prayer, and often do not need words, or at least not many words.

The tax collector addresses God with one of the

briefest and most touching prayers of the New Testament. According to the original Greek he says this: "God, be merciful to me, a sinner!" (Lk 18:13). The tax collector not only asks that God have mercy on him, but that he discharge the debt that he is no condition to expiate on his own. For the Jewish mentality of the time, every sin is a debt contracted and to be expiated. To render the idea, the evangelist Matthew tells the parable of the merciful master to whom the first slave owes ten thousand talents (Mt 18:24): a debt so exorbitant that a lifetime is not long enough to pay it off. Before God we are all debtors, and no one is in the black! The publican's short and sincere prayer reveals this disarming truth. Only the compassionate mercy of God can justify the publican, not the righteousness acquired before Him. In contrast with the prayer of the Pharisee, that of the publican says everything in very few gestures and words.

Conclusion

The parable of the Pharisee and the tax collector at the Temple has a surprise ending. Jesus exalts the reversal of the situation: while the tax collector returns home justified, the Pharisee is not justified. God alone knows and reads the human heart: He values it according to the sincerity and repentance with which one presents oneself before Him. Such a reversal of the situation is unthinkable for anyone. What becomes of the divine Law and the commandments that God has given to

His people? Doesn't the Law say that one must pay taxes, and tithes on one's increase? Isn't fasting one of the most widespread practices of piety among the Jewish people? With the reversal of the situation between the Pharisee and the tax collector, doesn't one run the risk of being a transgressor of the Law, even though one is justified and sanctified by God?

The parable of the Pharisee and the tax collector throws open a window onto the infinite mercy of God, who seeks a humble and repentant heart, not a strutting and arrogant man. The more one is a man or woman of prayer, the more humble one is, as in the *Magnificat* Mary recognizes the unexpected action of God: He scatters the proud in the imagination of their hearts and exalts the humble (Lk 1:51–52).

The Parable of the Fig Tree and the Approach of the Kingdom (Lk 2:29-36)

One of the typical traits of prayer that Jesus taught to His disciples is vigilance. The parable of the fig tree matches up with this requirement and is the last parable on prayer, since, among other things, Jesus exhorts the disciples to "stay awake at all times, praying" (Lk 21:36). The parable of the fig tree is among the shortest that Jesus told (Lk 21:29–31): just three verses dedicated to a fig tree that is about to blossom. The occasion allows Jesus to note that the kingdom of God is approaching like summer for a fig tree that is about to blossom. The parable is centered on the kingdom of God: how is one to recognize it? What are the signs that anticipate its presence? And how does vigilant prayer keep one from falling into the slumber of reason?

The relationship between the fig tree, ready to blossom for the summer, and the approach of the kingdom of God or of heaven, refers to the second petition of the Our Father: "Your kingdom come" (Lk 11:2). On the one hand, the disciple asks that the Lord bring His kingdom near; on the other, Jesus asks the disciple to learn to recognize the signs of the times regarding the nearness of the kingdom. Once again, Jesus illustrates the Our Father with parables about prayer.

The signs of the times

During the few years of His preaching in Galilee, Jesus proclaimed above all the approach of the kingdom of God. Sent to proclaim the kingdom of God (Lk 4:43), Jesus made it present with the selection of His disciples, with parables and the healing of the sick. Compared to a mustard seed (Lk 13:18–19) or to the yeast used to ferment dough (Lk 13:20–21), the kingdom of God is not visible to the naked eye, but requires a gaze that goes beyond. In practice, in order to recognize the kingdom of God in action it is necessary to look past the visible.

The community of disciples or the Church is the most tangible manifestation of the kingdom of God that Jesus proclaimed in words and deeds. It is appropriate to clarify that the Church is not the kingdom of God, but manifests it through the communion of those who continue to follow Jesus. It would be unfortunate to conflate the kingdom of God with the Church: there are too many failures on the part of the disciples to fall into this illusion. And yet the disciples who make up the Church manifest the kingdom of God with their communion and mission. Between the kingdom of God and the Church there is an intimate relationship, of tensions and congruities. But still, the kingdom of God has drawn near with the mission of Jesus, continues to reveal itself among the disciples in the Church, and awaits them until the final encounter with the Lord Jesus Christ. To teach His disciples to wait for the kingdom of God, Jesus tells, among other things, the parable of the fig tree.

Some of the symbols that run through the Bible are not chosen at random: one could think of the vine with the vineyard and the olive tree with the oil. Selected to represent the chosen people, the vineyard requires constant care from planting to harvest. Few plantations are as precious as an olive grove and the production of oil: it is the plant of election, since the oil is used for consecration. Even the fig tree with its fruit refers to the relationship between God and human beings. When the fig begins to blossom, it means that spring is turning to summer. Resting beneath a fig tree, as Nathanael did (Jn 1:47–48), means awaiting the signs of the times for the approach of the kingdom of God.

With its richness and beauty, creation always points to the Creator: human beings have the responsibility of recognizing the way in which creation harks back to the Creator. In bearing fruit in the good and in suffering abuse in the evil, creation maintains its relationship with the human person. Regarding the interconnection between creation and human beings, what St Paul states in the Letter to the Romans is revealing: "For the creation was subjected to futility, not willingly, but because of him who subjected it, in hope that the creation itself will be set free from its bondage to corruption and obtain the freedom of the glory of the children of God" (Rom 8:20–21). There is a profound co-participation between creation, human beings and believers that is expressed with what are called the "signs of the times." *Gaudium et Spes* of the Second Vatican Council attributed supreme importance to the relationships between the Church and the signs of the times: "The Church has always had the duty of scrutinizing the signs of the times and of interpreting them in the light of the Gospel. Thus, in language intelligible to each generation, she can respond to the perennial questions which men ask about this present life and the life to come, and about the relationship of the one to the other" (*Gaudium et Spes*, 4).

Vigilant prayer

In the context of the parable of the fig tree, between one season and another, Jesus urges the disciples to be vigilant, praying at all times (Lk 21:36). If at the beginning of the journey to Jerusalem the disciples asked Him to teach them to pray, it is because Jesus often kept vigil in prayer.

It is no coincidence that the choosing of the Twelve begins with Jesus' prayer through the night, until the morning (Lk 6:12–16). The epilogue of His mission also takes place in prayer, during His agony in Gethsemane (Lk 22:39–46). The terrible days of the passion saw Jesus coming and going between the Mount of Olives and the Temple of Jerusalem (Lk 21:37). If during the day He remained in the Temple to dialogue with the people, at night Jesus went to the Mount of Olives to drop everything else and strengthen His relationship with the Father more and more.

The disciples did not have the strength nor the courage to keep watch with Him, and were overcome by sleep. During the agony of Gethsemane, Jesus asked the disciples several times to be vigilant so as not to enter into temptation (Lk 22:40, 46). On this occasion, more than on others, instead of asking the Father not to abandon him in temptation the disciple must ask not to enter into it, because he finds himself with no way out when he is unable to keep watch with prayer. Between the sleep of reason and vigilant prayer, the disciple is forced to choose which side to take. If he opts for sleep, he is overcome with sadness or the loss of courage for discipleship. If he chooses to keep watch, he is in a position to recognize the signs of the times that he glimpses in creation and in society.

Between sleeping and keeping watch the disciple learns to go through the last phase of prayer as taught by Jesus. Vigilance in prayer is necessary because it reveals the face of hope. Keeping watch comes from hope, without which it doesn't make sense to keep watch through the night. But a few clarifications are necessary regarding hope; otherwise its nature will be misunderstood. Holy Scripture is the chief codex of hope for the Jewish people and the Christian community. It is no coincidence that Abraham, the father of faith, is at the same time the model of hope against all hope. There is a world of difference between hope in Western culture and the hope conveyed by the Bible. Just compare the myth of Pandora with any page of Scripture to note the differences. According to Greek myth, when Pandora has spilled all the evils into the world, at the bottom of the box there remains only the hope that is destined to go from illusion to fatal disappointment. With *Waiting for Godot,* Samuel Beckett represented better than anyone else what hope is for Western culture: two beggars waiting for a puny god who never shows up.

On the contrary, Scripture proclaims a different hope, based on an event and not on human desire: the exodus from Egypt is the paradigm of Jewish hope, and the Risen Lord is the ultimate reason for Christian hope. Between those who have no hope and those who believe, a hope stands forth which, rooted in faith and love, becomes a conviction that earthly life has a hereafter. If one of the first confessions of Christian faith is *Marana tha* ("The Lord comes" or "Come, Lord"), it is because the Word became flesh and believers contemplate His glory until life ends.

Vigilant prayer allows believers to choose what endures and not what passes. Without diminishing in any way the value of the realities in the world, vigilant prayer is recognized by the willingness to meet the Lord who comes. The brief parable of the fig tree teaches disciples to recognize the signs of the times and of the world in order to be in a condition to unpack them in light of the hereafter.

Conclusion

The last parable of Jesus in the Gospel of Luke is dedicated to vigilant prayer: this is the most mature phase of prayer. Here we ask the Father that "His kingdom come," or that He make His presence near in creation and in humanity. The disciple is presented with a choice between vigilance and sleep in the test that faith entails. Jesus did not face the hour of agony by sleeping through peaceful nights, but with vigilant prayer permeated with the invocation "Abba, Father" (Mk 14:36).

The more mature he is in the vigilance of prayer, the more the disciple realizes when a new season arrives for nature and for human beings. It seems that the charism of prophecy is increasingly rare in the Church of our time. This may correspond to the reality, but it is a scarcity that depends not on the Spirit's lack of generosity, but rather on the absence of vigilant prayer. Jesus' shortest parable ends with its focus on hope. An illusory and disappointed hope is contrasted with the hope rooted in the event of the death and resurrection of Jesus Christ. Christian hope is not one virtue among many, but Christ himself, the "hope of glory" (Col 1:27).

Conclusion

Jesus taught prayer by praying! This is the essential core of His teaching on prayer. The Our Father is the manifesto of prayer for every disciple. The combination of the Our Father and parables on prayer is original. On the one hand, the Our Father is the common thread of prayer in the parables; on the other, some of the parables explain the Our Father. In the light of the parables on prayer it is possible to delineate five phases of the original school of prayer taught by Jesus.

1. The parable of the troublesome friend teaches the transition from prayer dictated by urgency or necessity to prayer generated by the Holy Spirit. Prayer is like the vital bread that the Father gives to His children. Along with the Spirit, the Father gives each disciple what is necessary.

2. The second phase of prayer as taught by Jesus sees the compelling relationship between the merciful father and the two sons. One must always learn to ask for the forgiveness of one's debts without forget-

ting the forgiveness of one's debtors. God is always a Father in search of His children. With His mercy He corrects the prayer dictated by the urgency of the younger son, sanctifying it with His compassion and that of the elder, thus re-establishing their brotherhood. One cannot invoke God as Father if one does not recognize the other as brother.

3. The turning point in Jesus' school of prayer comes with the parable of the widow and the unbelieving judge. The petition not to enter into temptation, in the Our Father, is illustrated by the widow's persevering or constant faith. At issue is not any sort of moral temptation, but that of faith forced to go through the test.

4. Between profanation and sanctification of the name of God, the parable of the Pharisee and the tax collector at the Temple contrasts two types of prayer. On the one hand, the arrogant and narcissistic prayer of the Pharisee, and on the other the humble prayer of the tax collector. The reversal of the situation demonstrates that God justifies or sanctifies the tax collector and not the Pharisee.

5. The short and incisive parable of the blossoming fig tree closes the parables on prayer. Prayer reaches full maturity when, through vigilance, it allows the disciple to recognize the signs of the times or of the approaching kingdom of God. Between the

> Spirit who continues to guide believers and the kingdom to be recognized in the change of the seasons, prayer is more necessary than ever. Otherwise one is not in a position to recognize the different seasons of personal and community life. It is not by chance that the last phase of Jesus' school of prayer ends with vigilance open to hope, in view of the encounter with the Lord.

Pilgrims of hope is the motto of the next Jubilee for the Church in 2025. To the extent that prayer assists in the recognition of the signs of the times, the hope of believers is based on the encounter with Christ. The Christian life begins when the Master summons the disciple to follow Him; the epilogue is to go to meet Him in the lively hope of remaining with Him forever.

In preparation for the Jubilee Year 2025, the Exploring Prayer series delves into the various dimensions of prayer in the Christian life. These brief, accessible books can help you learn to dialogue with God and rediscover the beauty of trusting in the Lord with humility and joy.

Prayer Today: A Challenge to Overcome
Notes on Prayer: Volume 1
by Angelo Comastri
In order to have saints, what is needed are people of authentic prayer, and authentic prayer is that which inflames with a fire of love. Only in this way is it possible to lift the world and bring it near to the heart of God. To pray in truth, we must present ourselves before God with the open wounds of our smallness and our sin. Only in this way will the encounter with God be an encounter of liberation and redemption.

Praying with the Psalms
Notes on Prayer: Volume 2
by Gianfranco Ravasi
This little guide to the Psalms includes four cardinal points: a general reflection on prayer, the breath of the soul; a panoramic look at the psalmic texts; a portrait of the two protagonists, God and the worshipper, but also the intrusion of the presence of evil; and finally, an anthology of brief commentaries on the Psalms most dear to tradition and the liturgy. The hope is that all the faithful may draw fully from this wonderful treasury of prayers.

The Jesus Prayer
Notes on Prayer: Volume 3
by Juan Lopez Vergara
This book explores the unique experience of the fatherhood of God for Jesus Christ, whom he calls Abba — which in his native Aramaic language means "Dad." Throughout his earthly life, Jesus is in contact dialogue with Abba. From his Baptism in the Jordan through his public ministry and ultimately his crucifixion, this relationship will mark him forever, transforming his life, and our lives, too.

Praying with Saints and Sinners
Notes on Prayer: Volume 4
by Paul Brendan Murray
The saints whose writings on prayer and meditation

are explored in this book are among the most celebrated in the great spiritual tradition. The aim of this book is to discover what help the great saints can offer those of us who desire to make progress in the life of prayer, but who find ourselves being constantly deflected from our purpose, our tentative efforts undermined perhaps most of all by human weakness.

Parables on Prayer
Notes on Prayer: Volume 5
by Anthony Pitta
What characterizes, in a singular way, Jesus's teaching on prayer is the recourse to parables. Jesus did not invent a new system for praying. Jesus was not a hermit, a Buddhist monk, or a yogi. He instead chose the daily life of his people to teach prayer with parables. This book explores the parables in the Gospels explicitly related to prayer. The reader is guided by Jesus, the original teacher of prayer with parables.

The Church in Prayer
Notes on Prayer: Volume 6
by Carthusian Monks
Carthusian Monks reside in several international monasteries. Founded in 1084 by Saint Bruno, the Order of Carthusians are dedicated to prayer, in silence, in community. Like other cloistered religious, the Carthusians live a life focused on prayer and contemplation.

The Prayer of Mary and the Saints
Notes on Prayer: Volume 7
by Catherine Aubin
When Mary appears, anywhere in the whole world, the places where she appears have points in common with the biblical places where she stayed and lived. This book reviews these places, examining what they reveal to us about Mary's identity, and what the inner spaces are that Mary asks us to dwell in today. This book also explores the unique relationship two holy women each had with Mary, leading us toward a new, deep revelation of Mary's closeness to each of us.

The Prayer Jesus Taught Us: The "Our Father"
Notes on Prayer: Volume 8
by Hugh Vanni
This book identifies the theological-biblical structure underlying the Lord's Prayer and situates it in the living environment of the early Church. This will give us a framework of reference, and as a result we will see first the antecedents in Mark, then the systematic presentation of Matthew, Paul's push forward, the accentuation of Luke, and, finally, the mature synthesis found in John.